The Bible Tells Me So:

New Testament Stories for Children

written by Victoria Fletcher

illustrated by Emery Reid

ISBN: 978-1-7340868-4-3

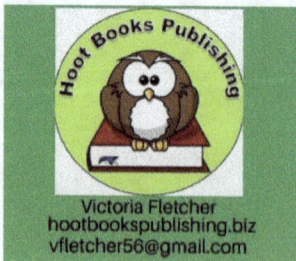

Victoria Fletcher
hootbookspublishing.biz
vfletcher56@gmail.com

Hello Bible story readers,

I hope you will enjoy these Bible stories from the New Testament. I loved Bible stories when I was growing up and loved to tell them to the children I taught at church and Vacation Bible School. They offer so many examples of how we should live in order to bring honor and glory to our Lord Jesus Christ. I have enjoyed writing these stories and hope they will be different than ones you have read before. I hope that you will enjoy them and share them with others. I'd like to let you in on a hint about finding the references listed for the stories that a Sunday School teacher of mine taught me when I was young. When looking for the book of the Bible, they use a dash to show chapters and a colon to show chapter and verse. Here is an example from my favorite Bible book: Esther 1-2 (means Esther chapters 1 and 2) Esther 1:2 (means Esther chapter 1 verse 2).

I wish you many years of enjoying these Bible stories and passing them on to children of your own. May God richly bless you in your life.

Your Friend in Him,

Vicki Fletcher

Dedication

I would like to dedicate this book in memory of my mother, Patsie A. Fletcher and in honor of my father, James R. Fletcher. They were the Christian parents that helped me grow up and love the Lord and want to serve Him with any talents He has blessed me with.

Table of Contents

A Witness to the Light:
John the Baptist
Background- Luke 1:5-25, 39-45,
57-66; John 1:1-18

In the days of King Herod of
Judea, there was a priest named
Zacharias and his wife Elisabeth. One
day in the temple, Zacharias asked
God to give him a son. Gabriel, an
angel of the Lord, appeared to
Zacharias and told him that his prayer
had been heard and God was going to
send him a son. Gabriel told Zacharias
that he was to name his son, John.
Zacharias replied, "But we have no one
in our family by that name." Gabriel
told Zacharias that he would be
stricken dumb (unable to speak) until
his son was born and he was named
John. Your son will be filled with the
Holy Ghost from the time he is in

1

Elisabeth's womb. He will be a witness to the Savior, the Light of the World. Gabriel told Zacharias that he would also be bringing news of the baby Jesus' birth to Elisabeth's cousin Mary. Read the next story to learn more about Gabriel's message to Mary.

Memory Verse- Matthew 7:7

Ask and it shall be given you; seek and ye shall find; knock and it shall be opened unto you.

Application for Life:

Zacharias was a priest in the temple. He believed in God and lived a life as a servant of Him. I bet even Zacharias was surprised to see Gabriel in the temple with a message from God that God was answering Zacharias' prayer for a son. Wow!!! God is so gracious and merciful to answer our prayers. If we ask Him, seek Him, and live our lives for Him, He is ready to answer our prayers, too. Just remember that sometimes God doesn't answer with exactly what <u>we</u> ask or want but by what **He** knows is best for us.

Good News: The Birth of Jesus

Background- Matthew 1:18-25;
Luke 1:26-38, 2:1-40

Gabriel, an angel of the Lord, went to the town of Nazareth. He appeared to a young virgin girl named Mary who was engaged to be married to Joseph. Gabriel told Mary, "Thou art highly favored: the Lord is with thee. Blessed art thou among women." Mary was afraid when she saw the angel. Gabriel told her not to be afraid. "You will have a child, sent by God, and you will call him Jesus because He will be the Savior of the world."

When Joseph found out that Mary was with child, he was going to send her away without anyone finding out. Gabriel spoke to Joseph in a dream and told him not to be afraid to

4

marry Mary because this was God's Son sent to earth by God. Joseph married Mary. They had to travel to Bethlehem to pay taxes. The town was crowded because of all the taxpayers. Everywhere they stopped, they were told there was no room for them. One owner of an inn told them they could spend the night in his stable. In that humble stable, our precious Lord and Savior, Jesus Christ was born.

Gabriel and a host of angels appeared to some shepherds in the field. The shepherds were terrified (bet you saw that coming). Gabriel said, "Do not be afraid. God has sent His Son to earth. He is in a stable in Bethlehem. Go and worship Him." The shepherds left and went to Bethlehem. When they arrived at the stable, they saw baby Jesus lying in a manger. Mary and Joseph were beside Him. The shepherds bowed at the manger and worshipped the tiny baby Jesus, the Savior of the World.

Memory Verse- Luke 2:11

For unto you is born this day in the city of David, a Savior, which is Christ the Lord.

Application for Life:

Gabriel was sure one busy angel. What a great job he had getting to announce the births to people. We are so lucky that God loved us enough to send His only Son to come to the world He created to save us from our sins. Thank you, God, for this special gift.

Gifts for a King
Background- Matthew 2

After the birth of Jesus, wise men (sometimes called the Magi) followed the star in the east to come to worship baby Jesus. King Herod heard about the new king. He was very troubled. He wanted the wise men to find the baby and come back to tell him where the baby was. King Herod told them it was so he could go and worship Him, but King Herod really wanted to kill baby Jesus.

The wise men found the young boy Jesus. They presented him with gifts of gold, frankincense, and myrrh. God warned them in a dream not to go back to Herod but return home another way. An angel of the Lord told Joseph in a dream to take Mary and Jesus and flee to Egypt because

King Herod wanted to kill Jesus. They stayed in Egypt until King Herod died. Then they returned to their home in Nazareth to live.

Memory Verse- 2 Corinthians 9:15

Thanks be unto God for His unspeakable gift.

Application for Life:

The gifts from the wise men might seem strange but I believe they were symbols of the role that Jesus would play in the world- prophet, priest, and king. Remember to bring your gifts to Jesus even today. We should give of our time, talents, and tithes to thank Jesus for what He did for us and how He is always interceding for us to God, His Father, every day of our lives.

John the Baptist
Prepares the Way
Background- Matthew 3:1-17;
Mark 1:1-11; Luke 3:1-22

John was born to Zacharias and Elisabeth a few months before baby Jesus was born. John was sent to prepare people to accept Jesus as the Son of God.

John preached and baptized in the wilderness. He ate honey and locusts and wore camel skins.

John told the people that there would come one whose shoelaces John would not be worthy to tie. John was speaking of Jesus, the Messiah.

Jesus came out of Nazareth down to Galilee where John was preaching. When John saw Him, he said, "This is the One of whom I spoke."

11

Jesus asked John to baptize him. John said that he was not worthy, and Jesus should baptize him instead. Jesus said that He wanted to be obedient to His Father, God, and be baptized. When John baptized Jesus, a dove descended and a voice from heaven said, "This is my beloved Son, in whom I am well pleased."

Memory Verse- John 1:7

The same came for a witness, to bear witness of the Light, that all men through him might believe.

Application for Life:

God was pleased with His Son Jesus because Jesus had been obedient. When we are saved by Jesus Christ, God wants us to be obedient and follow Him in baptism. Baptism doesn't mean you're saved. Baptism is a symbol of obedience to God to show others that we have accepted Jesus as our personal Lord and Savior. Just like John, God wants us to be witnesses of the Light of the World. I hope you've already accepted Jesus and been baptized. If not, I'll pray that you will make that decision soon.

The Temptation of Jesus

Background- Matthew 4:1-11;
Mark 1:12-13; Luke 4:1-15

Immediately after Jesus was baptized, the Spirit drove Him into the wilderness. Jesus fasted for 40 days and nights. Afterward, He was hungry. Satan came to him and tempted Him. "Turn these stones to bread and eat," Satan implored. Jesus responded, "It is written, man shall not live by bread alone but by every word that proceedeth out of the mouth of God." Satan took Jesus to the Holy City and sat Him on a pinnacle of the temple. Satan told Jesus to jump off the pinnacle because the angels would not let Him get hurt. Jesus said, "Thou shalt not tempt the Lord thy God." Satan then took Jesus to a tall mountain where they could see the kingdoms of the world. Satan spoke again to Jesus and said, "I will give You all these things if You will fall down and worship me." Jesus said, "Get behind me, Satan. Don't you know that you should only worship the Lord thy God and only serve Him." I bet Jesus was thinking, "Excuse me, but my Father, God, has already given me all these things." Satan gave up and left. The angels came and took care of Jesus.

Memory Verse- Luke 11:4b

And lead us not into temptation but deliver us from evil.

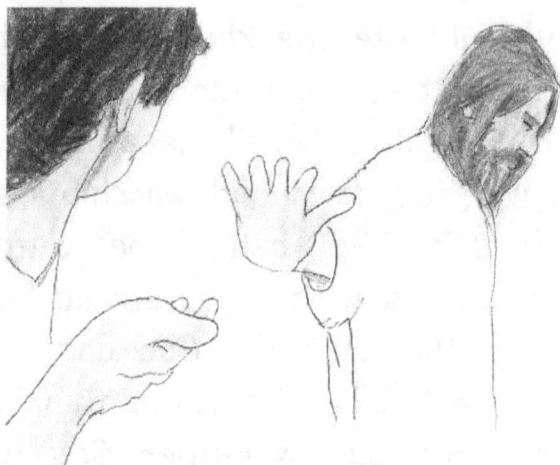

Application for Life:

Satan tempts us daily with everything he can. He knows our desires, wishes, and weaknesses. He uses them against us. Your heart knows right from wrong. Listen to your heart. The only way to fight temptation is to try to stay in God's Word, pray, and live for Him each day. You'll be rewarded when you follow Him.

The Disciples

Background- Matthew 4:18-22, 9:9-
13; Mark 1:16-20, 2:13-17, 3:13-17;
Luke 5:27-32, 6:12-16; John 1:35-51

Jesus was walking by the Sea of
Galilee when He saw some fishermen
casting their nets into the sea. Jesus
said, "Come follow me and I will make
you fishers of men." Andrew and his
brother Simon Peter left their fishing
nets and followed Jesus. Jesus
changed Simon Peter's name to Cephas
which meant stone. James and John,
also fishermen, followed Jesus, too.
These were the first four disciples of
Jesus. Jesus also called Levi the tax
collector which he named Matthew.
The other disciples were Phillip,
Bartholomew, Thomas, James son of
Alphaeus, Thaddaeus, Simon the
Canaanite, and Judas Iscariot. Jesus
and the twelve disciples went to the

mountain where Jesus ordained them. The disciples were given the power by Jesus to preach, heal people, and cast out demons from people. Everywhere Jesus and his disciples went, large multitudes of people came to hear them speak and to be healed.

Memory Verse- 3 John 11

Beloved, follow not that which is evil, but that which is good. He that doeth good is of God: but he that doeth evil hath not seen God.

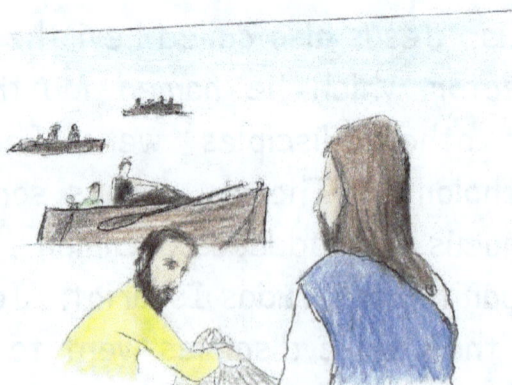

Application for Life:

If you have accepted Jesus as your Savior and Lord, then you are now one of His disciples. We may not have the power to preach or heal but we can be witnesses for Jesus. We can tell others what Jesus means in our lives and what He can do for them. There are so many beliefs and religions in this world but there is still only ONE GOD who sent His Son Jesus to take our place so we wouldn't have to die from our sins. The world needs to know the One, True God and His precious Son, our Savior, Jesus Christ.

Jesus' First Miracle
Background- John 2:1-12

Jesus, His disciples, and His mother Mary went to a wedding in Cana of Galilee. During the wedding, the host ran out of wine to serve the guests. Jesus saw six water pots of stone. He told His disciples to fill them with water. The disciples filled each stone pot to the brim with water. Jesus told the disciples to draw out of the pot and take it to the host. The host called the groom over and asked him why he had saved the very best wine for the end of the ceremony. "This is wonderful wine. I don't understand. Most people use the best wine at the beginning of the ceremony and use the rest at the end." The groom replied, "I do not know where this wine came from."

The host or the groom did not know where the wine came from, but the disciples did. Jesus had turned the water in the pots into the best wine they had ever tasted. This was the first of many miracles that Jesus would show His disciples and the people.

Memory Verse- Psalm 86:10

For Thou art great and doest wondrous things: Thou art God alone.

Application for Life:

I have attended weddings before but never where a miracle was performed especially by Jesus Himself. We will be part of the grandest wedding ever one day. Jesus, the groom, will come for His bride-- Christians who have accepted Him as their Savior and Lord. On that day, His bride will join Him in heaven and live in the glory of God and His Son Jesus forevermore. Don't get left out of this glorious day. Be sure Jesus is your Savior. If I don't get to meet you here on earth, I'll see you in glory one day.

Nicodemus
Background- John 3:1-22

One day, a Pharisee, a ruler of the Jews, went to see Jesus. His name was Nicodemus. Nicodemus talked to Jesus. He said, "Rabbi (which is Jewish for teacher), I know from your miracles and teachings that God has sent you." Jesus replied, "Yes, God sent me and unless you are born again, you cannot see the kingdom of heaven." Nicodemus was startled. "But Rabbi, I cannot go back into my mother's womb and be born again. Why do you ask this of me?" Jesus explained to Nicodemus that being born again was through the Living Water and the Holy Spirit. When the Holy Spirit lives in you, then you will be able to see the kingdom of heaven one day.

Nicodemus was having trouble understanding even though he was a Jewish teacher himself. Jesus explained to him how to be saved. Imagine getting to hear the salvation story from Jesus Himself. Nicodemus was a lucky man to come to know Jesus this way.

Memory Verse- John 3:16

For God so loved the world that He gave His only begotten Son that whosoever believeth in Him shall not perish but have everlasting life.

Application for Life:

John 3:16 was turned into a Valentine not long ago. I think it is appropriate since it is God's love sent to us. Here is the verse as a valentine. Share it with others.

For God so lo<u>V</u>ed the world

th<u>A</u>t He gave

His on<u>L</u>y begotten Son

that whoso<u>E</u>ver believeth

i<u>N</u> Him

shall no<u>T</u>

per<u>I</u>ish but have

everlasti<u>N</u>g

lif<u>E</u>

The Woman at the Well
Background- John 4:1-38

Jesus had been preaching in Judea. He was going back to Galilee and had to pass through Samaria. Jesus stopped in the town of Sychar at Jacob's well to get a drink since He was thirsty from the long journey. He sent the disciples into the city to buy some food.

A woman came to the well. Jesus asked her for a drink. The woman was shocked. "Why do you ask me for a drink when Jews and Samaritans have nothing to do with each other," asked the Samaritan woman. Jesus told her that if she knew who He was, she could have asked for the Living Water. "Please give me of the water where I will never thirst again," she replied. Jesus said, "Go and call thy husband and come back to me." The woman answered, "I have no husband." Jesus said, "You told the truth. You have had five husbands. The man you are with now is not your husband." The woman gasped. "Are you a prophet or the Messiah?" she questioned. Jesus said, "I am the Messiah of whom you speak." The woman ran to the city to tell everyone to come and meet Jesus who had told her everything she had ever done. He shared with me how to have the Living Water. Many other Samaritans believed because of the Samaritan's woman's testimony.

Memory Verse- Revelation 22:17b

And whosoever will, let him take the water of life freely.

Application for Life:

Just as Jesus told Nicodemus and the Samaritan woman, we must accept the Living Water in order to have eternal life in heaven with God the Father and Jesus His Son. I hope you've already received this free gift. If you haven't, I hope you will soon. I want to be in eternity with you, my dear friend.

Jesus Heals

Background- Matthew 8:1-4, 14-17, 28-34; 9:1-8, 27-34; 15:21-28; 17:14-21, 20:29-3; Mark 1:21-34, 40-45; 2:1-12, 5:1-20; 7:24-37; 8:22-26; 9:14-29; 10:46-52; Luke 4:31-41; 5:12-26; 8:26-39; 9:27-43; John 4:46-54; 5:1-15; 9:1-34

During Jesus' life on earth, He healed many people. He had great compassion on those who came to Him asking to be healed. Below are several examples of the healing power of Jesus. I have listed them in types of healing:

❖ Paralyzed- Four friends brought their paralyzed friend to Jesus to be healed. There were so many people that they couldn't get in. They took the paralyzed man to the roof and lowered him down to Jesus. Jesus said, "I can see how you have faith." Jesus healed the paralyzed man. The crowd was amazed and glorified God.

❖ Lame- There was a man in Bethesda that had been lame for 38 years. He had no one to help him get to the pool that the angel came to that healed people. Jesus asked him if he wanted to be whole. The man told Jesus he had no one to help him into the pool. Jesus said, "Rise, take up thy bed and walk." The man immediately rose and walked.

❖ Blind- Two blind men cried out to Jesus to have mercy on them. Jesus asked them if they believed He could heal them, and they said yes. Jesus touched their eyes, and they could see. Another blind man, named

Bartimaeus, of Bethsaida, asked to be healed. Jesus spat in His hands and put His hands on the man's eyes. The man's eyes were opened. Also, a man's eyes were restored when Jesus put clay on them and told the man to wash in the pool of Siloam.

❖ Demon-possessed- Two men that were demon-possessed came out of the tombs to stop Jesus and the disciples from passing. Jesus commanded the demons to go into some pigs nearby. The pigs ran violently over a steep mountain and died in the waters below. Another man asked Jesus to heal his son. "My son falls into the fire and water. The disciples could not heal him," the man told Jesus. Jesus rebuked the demon, and the boy was healed.

- ❖ Deaf/Dumb (unable to speak) - In Decapolis, a deaf and mute man was brought to be healed. Jesus spat, put His finger to His tongue, and then to the man's ears. The man could hear and speak. The people that witnessed it were amazed.
- ❖ Leprosy- In Galilee, Jesus healed a man with leprosy. The man said to Jesus, "If Thou wilt, Thou can make me whole." Jesus replied, "I will. Be thou clean."
- ❖ Sicknesses- A woman had a blood disease all of her life. She touched the robe of Jesus and was healed instantly. One man's son in Capernaum was sick. The man asked Jesus to heal him. Jesus told the man to go home that his son was healed. Jesus healed his disciple Peter's mother-in-law who had been sick in bed with a fever. She

immediately   arose   and ministered to Jesus and the disciples. One woman's daughter was healed in Canaan because she had great faith.

Memory Verse- Malachi 4:2a

But unto you that fear My name shall the Son of righteousness arise with healing in his wings.

Application for Life:

I have been a witness to healing through the power of prayer. Jesus is still performing His healing miracles for us on earth if we have faith in Him and pray to Him and ask for His healing touch. Sometimes people still die even though we pray. We must remember that God knows every person's life and death before we are even born. We must continue to pray for what we want but trust God to do what we need, even if it is sometimes losing someone we love. Only God knows the reason. We can ask Him in heaven what that reason was if it isn't revealed to us while we are here on earth. God is the Great Physician. He delights in His children asking Him in prayer to take away the sicknesses we have here on earth.

Sermon on the Mount

Background- Matthew 5:1-12;
Luke 6:17-23

One day after Jesus had been preaching to the crowds, He went up on the mountain and called His 12 disciples to come with Him. There Jesus taught the disciples with His message, called the Sermon on the Mount. Jesus used the word blessed but I am going to call it fortunate so you might better understand the message:

* ❖ Humble men are fortunate because they will see the kingdom of heaven.
* ❖ Those who mourn are fortunate because they will be comforted.
* ❖ The meek and lowly are fortunate because they will be given the whole earth.

- ❖ Those who long to be good and just are fortunate because they will be completely satisfied.
- ❖ Those who are merciful and kind are fortunate because they will be shown mercy.
- ❖ Those with pure hearts are fortunate because they will see God.
- ❖ Those who strive for peace are fortunate because they will be called the Sons of God.
- ❖ Those who are persecuted because they are good are fortunate because they will have the kingdom of heaven.
- ❖ Those who are persecuted, reviled, and lied about because they follow Jesus will be rewarded greatly in heaven.

Memory Verse- Ephesians 1:3

Blessed be the God and Father of our Lord Jesus Christ who hath blessed us with all spiritual blessings in heavenly places in Christ.

Application for Life:

All of the blessings that Jesus spoke of in the Sermon on the Mount can be ours, too. If we believe in Jesus, follow Him, obey His Word, work to become good and pure and righteous, and stand up for Him here on earth, we will have great riches in heaven when He calls us home one day. Those rewards in heaven are definitely a reason to walk with Jesus here on earth.

Faith of the Centurion

Background- Matthew 8:5-13;
Luke 7:1-10

Just after Jesus had healed a man with leprosy, He went to Capernaum. When He was there, a centurion (a Roman army captain) came to him. The centurion wanted Jesus to come to his home and heal his servant boy who was paralyzed and in pain. Jesus said, "Yes, I will come with you and heal the boy." The centurion said, "Lord, I am not worthy that you come to my house. If you will just speak the word, my servant boy will be healed." Jesus marveled at the faith and told His followers, "I haven't seen faith like this in all of Israel." Jesus told the centurion, "Go thy way. As you have believed, so be it done for you." The centurion's servant boy was healed that very hour.

Memory Verse- Matthew 17:20

And Jesus said unto them, because of your unbelief: for verily I say unto you, If ye have faith as a grain of mustard seed, ye shall say unto this mountain, remove hence to yonder place; and it shall remove, and nothing shall be impossible unto you.

Application for Life:

Faith is defined as believing without seeing. The centurion had faith and his servant was healed. I hope, if Jesus were here today, that He would see faith in me just like the centurion. Although I cannot see Jesus face to face while I am on earth, I can call to Him in prayer and He hears me. Be sure to pray to Him for any need, question, or guidance you have in your life. Have faith that He will answer you in the way that He knows is best.

Jesus Raises the Dead

Background- Matthew 9:18-26;
Mark 5:21-43; Luke 7:11-17, 8:40-56;
and John 11:1-44

When Jesus was on earth, He did all kinds of healing. Even more remarkable were His acts of raising someone to life after they had died. Here are three times when Jesus raised the dead:

❖ When Jesus and His followers got to a city called Nain, they were having a funeral. The young son, an only child of a widow, was being carried out of town. The widow was weeping. Jesus had compassion on her. He said, "Do not cry." Jesus went to the casket and said, "Young man, arise." The young man sat up and began to speak to those around him. Jesus took him back to his mother.

❖ Jairus, a ruler of a Jewish synagogue, came to Jesus and told him his daughter was dying. Jairus begged Jesus to come home with him and heal her. While they were on the way, a servant came to tell Jairus that his daughter was dead. Jesus said, "Don't be afraid. Trust me and she'll be alright." When they got to Jairus' house, Jesus told them that the little girl was not dead but asleep. The servants all laughed at Jesus. Jesus took the girl's hand and said, "Arise." The girl woke up and Jesus told them to get her some food.

❖ Jesus had 3 very dear friends that lived in Bethany. Mary and Martha sent word that their brother Lazarus was sick and wanted Jesus to come and heal him. When Jesus got there, Martha and Mary said, "If you had just been here sooner, Lazarus would not have died." Jesus told them, "Thy brother will rise again." Jesus went to the tomb where Lazarus was. Jesus cried for his friend. He said to take away the stone. Martha said, "Lord, it's been 4 days and he will stink." Jesus said, "If you believe, you will see the glory of God." Jesus cried out, "Lazarus, come forth." Lazarus came out of the tomb still wrapped in the cloths for burying. Jesus told them, "Unwrap the cloths and let him go." Many that saw this miracle believed in Jesus that day.

Memory Verse- John 11:35

Jesus wept.

Application for Life:

The memory verse for today is the shortest verse in the Bible (King James version). Jesus was sad that his friend had died but He already knew the plan to show God's glory. Martha and Mary couldn't believe Jesus wouldn't come sooner and heal their brother, Lazarus. They didn't understand what Jesus was going to do. What a glorious miracle that would have been to see Lazarus walking out of the tomb, alive again through Jesus! I hope you believe in Jesus as your Savior and Lord. If you do, when you die on this earth, you will be alive again through Jesus in heaven.

The Miracles of Jesus

Background- Matthew 8:23-27,
14:13-23, 14:34-36, 15:32-39;
Mark 4:35-41, 6:30-56, 8:1-10;
Luke 8:22-25, 9:10-17; John 6:1-21

While Jesus was on earth, He performed many miracles so that others could see the power of God. Here are a few of the miracles Jesus did:

❖ Calms the storm- Once when Jesus and His disciples were on a ship, there came a storm with terrible winds and waves. Jesus was asleep. The disciples woke him and asked Him if He cared that they were all going to drown from the storm. Jesus said to the wind and sea, "Peace, be still." The wind ceased and there was a great calm. Jesus asked the disciples, "Why were you afraid? Where is your faith?" The disciples were amazed at what Jesus had done. They said to each other, "Who is this man that even the winds and the sea obey him."

❖ Feeding the hungry- On 2 different occasions, Jesus fed multitudes of people with only a few loaves of bread and small fish. The first time, there was a group of 5000 men (more counting the women and children) that was fed with a small boy's lunch of 5 loaves of bread and 2 fish. After everyone was fed, the disciples took up 12 baskets of food left over. Another time, there were 4000 people. They were fed with 7 loaves and a few small fish. When they had finished eating,

7 baskets of leftover food was collected.

❖ Walking on water- Jesus sent his disciples on a ship while He went to the mountain alone to pray. During the night, He could see them having trouble rowing because of the winds. When the disciples looked out on the sea, they saw what they thought was a spirit walking on the water. Jesus spoke, "Don't be afraid. It is I." Jesus got on the boat and the wind ceased. The disciples were amazed.

Memory Verse- Psalm 29:4

The voice of the Lord is powerful: the voice of the Lord is full of majesty.

Application for Life:

Wouldn't it have been amazing to see Jesus perform miracles? I would have loved to see Him walking on water. We need to be aware of the miracles around us every day. I'm going to share a poem I wrote when I was 12 years old with you today. I think it shows the everyday miracles we sometimes forget to look at or remember. Hope you enjoy it.

A Rewarding Search

I started out on a search for God today 'cause a friend said he was dead.

Then seeing my bewildered look, he turned and walked away.

I just bowed my head, and I began to pray.

"Oh God," I said, "I don't believe this thing that he has said.

I know that You are living. I know that You're not dead.

But God, I pray, if there is a way

that I might see Your face among the beauty of the heavens today."

I saw the beauty of a tree. I heard a robin sing.

I saw the farmer plant the seed where soon the corn would be.

I heard the laughter of a child playing on a swing.

And then, off in the distance, I heard a church bell ring.

Later on, I thought about the miracle of birth

and about the soft, spring rain falling to the earth.

I saw a rainbow up above as I traveled on my way.

Oh God, I know You're living, I saw Your face today.

The Good Samaritan
Background- Luke 10:30-37

Many times when Jesus was teaching, He used parables (stories). Here is one Jesus used to teach people to love others.

One day, a Jew was traveling from Jerusalem to Jericho. He was robbed by thieves. They took his money and his clothes. They beat him until he was nearly dead and left him there by the side of the road. Later that day, a Jewish priest passed by. The priest saw the man and crossed to the other side of the road and went right on by. Soon after, a Jewish temple assistant saw the man. He passed him by as well. A little later, a Samaritan man came by. Jews and Samaritans didn't like each other. When the Samaritan man saw the

Jewish man, he was filled with compassion. The Samaritan man poured oil and wine on the wounds of the Jewish man and bound them. The Samaritan man put the Jewish man on his donkey, took him to an inn and cared for him. When the Samaritan needed to leave the next day, he gave the innkeeper money to care for the wounded man. "If this is not enough money, I will give you more as soon as I return" said the Samaritan man.

Jesus asked the people, "Which of these was a neighbor to the wounded man?" They answered, "The one who showed him mercy." Jesus said, "Go and do thou likewise."

Memory Verse- Luke 10:27

And He answering said, Thou shalt love the Lord thy God with all thy heart, with all thy soul, with all thy strength, and with all thy mind, and thy neighbor as thyself."

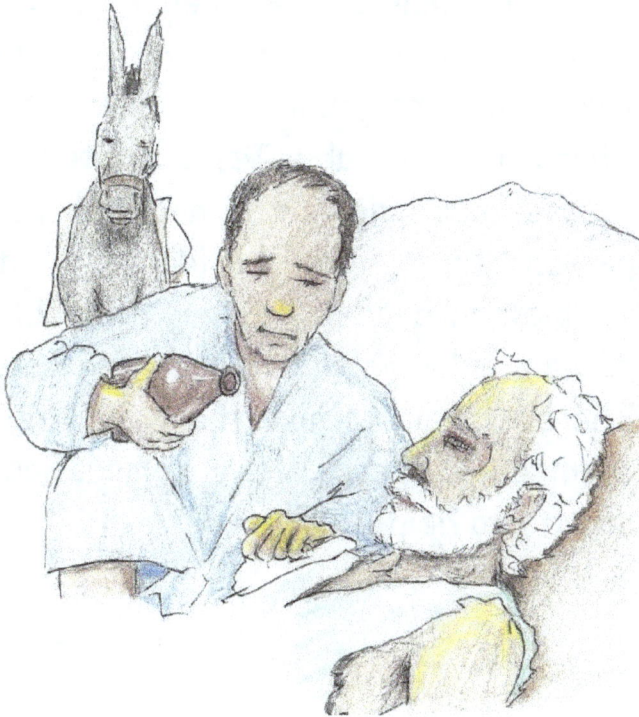

Application for Life:

I hope that I can show compassion for others like the good Samaritan man showed to the wounded Jewish man. Even though they were not friendly nations, the Samaritan man showed mercy. Jesus told us to love God first and then to love our neighbor as ourselves. Through this parable Jesus was telling us that our neighbor is not just the person that lives beside us but whomever we meet. We might be able to help a "neighbor" in need one day. The best help to give them is to tell them about Jesus, have compassion, and try to help their need.

The Prodigal Son
Background- Luke 15:11-32

Another parable of Jesus tells of love and forgiveness. It is about a man who had two sons. The younger son asked his father to give him his share of the money he would inherit so he could leave home. The father divided his money between his two sons. The younger son took off on his own. It was not very long that he found himself without anything because he had wasted it away partying every night. During this time, there was a famine in the land and the young man began to be hungry. He went to work for a man feeding his pigs. To let you know the young man was truly desperate, a Jew does not like to be close to a pig. They think they are unclean animals under the Jewish law.

While taking care of the pigs and even wanting to eat their food, the young man thought, "My father's servants eat well. I can return and ask if my father would let me be his servant." The father saw his young son coming. He ran to the young man, hugged him, and kissed him. The young son asked to become a servant. The father told one of his servants to bring a robe, a ring, shoes, and prepare a feast. "My son was lost but now is found," said the father. The oldest son was upset when he got home. "I have served thee every day and you have not given me a feast," the oldest son said angrily. His father said, "Son, everything I have is yours because you have always been with me. Your brother was lost but is now found; he was dead but now alive. That is why we are celebrating."

Memory Verse- Psalm 86:5

For Thou Lord art good and ready to forgive; and plenteous in mercy unto all them that call unto Thee.

Application for Life:

How many of you have brothers and sisters? Have you ever been jealous? Come on, be honest. We all get jealous of others at times- maybe they have the prettiest hair or clothes, the best car, the super job, the greatest house. We need to be thankful every day for everything God blesses us with. Don't take things for granted. Hold on to those you love- they are the most important gift you could ever receive.

The Rich Young Ruler
Background- Matthew 19:16-30;
Mark 10:17-31; Luke 18:18-30

One day a rich young ruler came to Jesus and asked, "Good Master, how can I have eternal life?" Jesus answered, "Why do you call Me good? There is only one that is good and that is God." Jesus asked the young man, "Do you keep the commandments?" The young man replied, "Yes, Lord, I have kept the commandments since I was a boy." Jesus said, "There is one more thing you need to do to enter the kingdom of God. Sell all that you own and give the money to the poor. Then come and follow Me." The young man went away very sad. He was very rich and did not want to part with his wealth. Jesus told His disciples, "It is easier for a camel to go through the eye of a needle than a rich man to go to heaven." Jesus ended this parable by telling His disciples that if people gave up their riches on earth to obey and serve Him that they would gain even more on earth and especially when they go to heaven.

Memory Verse- Mark 10:27b

With me, it is impossible, but not with God: for with God, all things are possible.

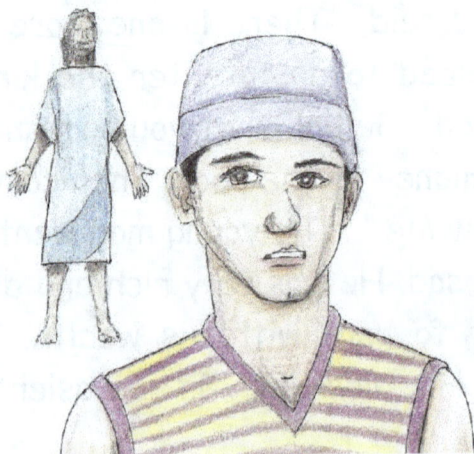

Application for Life:

How funny to think about a camel going through the eye of a needle. I hope the rich, young ruler decided to accept Jesus later on. I guess we'll only be able to find out when we get to heaven and ask if he is there. It doesn't mean that if we are wealthy we can't go to heaven. Jesus was trying to tell us that if we let <u>anything else</u> come before God that it would be very hard to be with Him in heaven. Even my wants here on earth cannot keep me from following God, obeying His commands, and serving Him because I know He gives me what I need. He will bless me with even more as I continue to live for Him. My greatest reward will be getting to spend eternity with Him in heaven.

Zacchaeus, the Wee Little Man

Background- Luke 19:1-10

Jesus traveled to Jericho one day. In the town, there lived a rich tax collector who was hated by the people because he cheated them out of their money. This man was named Zacchaeus. He was a short man and could not see Jesus as He was passing through the town. Zacchaeus decided to climb up in a nearby sycamore tree to get a better look. Imagine his surprise when Jesus stopped, looked up in the tree, and shouted, "Zacchaeus, come down from there. I'm going to go to your house to eat with you." Zacchaeus hurried down from the tree. He told Jesus he would give back the money he had cheated the people out of. Zacchaeus was saved that day. Jesus rejoiced. The people began talking among themselves saying, "Why would Jesus want to eat with a sinner?" Jesus spoke to the people and said, "The Son of Man is come to save the sinners who are lost."

Memory Verse- Luke 19:10

For the Son of Man is come to seek and to save that which is lost.

Application for Life:

I'm short just like Zacchaeus. I would probably have climbed a tree to get a look at Jesus, too. The best part of this story is that Jesus didn't care what Zacchaeus was (a cheater, greedy, sinner) but what he could become. After Jesus spent the day with Zacchaeus, he said he would return people's money that he cheated them out of. Zacchaeus wanted to make things right in his life because he met Jesus. We are so blessed that Jesus still wants us to be His children no matter what we have done but because of what we can become through His love and grace. Praise You Lord for taking my sins away and giving me eternal life with You some day.

The Triumphal Entry

Background- Matthew 21:1-11; Mark 11:1-11; Luke 19:28-40; John 12:12-19

When Jesus and His disciples had traveled to Bethphage and Bethany for the Passover (a Jewish feast), Jesus sent two of the disciples to go into the town and get a donkey colt for Him to ride on into town. The two disciples returned with the colt. As Jesus rode into town on the colt, the disciples and the crowd of people traveling with Jesus and from the town threw their garments in the street or waved palm branches. They shouted, "Hosanna. Blessed is He that comes in the name of the Lord." Some of the Pharisees told Jesus to make His followers be quiet. Jesus said, "If they do not cry out for me, then the rocks would cry out."

This was the first event of what people call the "Easter" story. The rest of the events of this story will follow. This was a very sad time for the followers of Jesus but such a wonderful gift to us that I must tell you "the rest of the story" as Paul Harvey would have said.

Memory Verse- Mark 11:9b

Hosanna. Blessed is He that cometh in the name of the Lord.

Application for Life:

The people were excited to go with Jesus from town to town. I can't blame them. Imagine getting to be near Jesus, hear Him preach, and see Him heal. Awesome!!! Jesus knew what He was about to face so He had to be sad. I'm so glad He was willing to do what God wanted Him to do for us even if it meant the agony He was about to face. Thank You Jesus for loving us all so much.

The Last Supper

Background- Matthew 26:17-19,
26-29; Mark 14:12-16, 22-25;
Luke 22:7-20

On the first day of the Passover, the disciples asked Jesus where they should go to prepare a meal for them to eat. Jesus told Peter and John to go to the city and ask a man to let them use his upper room. The disciples went to the man and he agreed so they prepared a meal in the upper room where they could eat. Jesus and His disciples gathered together. Jesus took the bread and broke it into pieces and gave a piece to His disciples. "This is my body which will be broken for you; eat it." Jesus took the wine and served it to His disciples. "This is my blood which will be shed for you; drink it." Jesus told the disciples that night that one of them was going to betray Him. The disciples argued and said they never would. They sang a hymn together and then they went to the Mount of Olives to pray.

Memory Verse- 1 Corinthians 11:24-25

And when He had given thanks, He brake it and said, "Take, eat: this is my body which is broken for you; this do in remembrance of Me." After the same manner also, He took the cup, when He had supped saying, "This cup is the new testament in My blood: this do ye, as oft as ye drink it, in remembrance of Me."

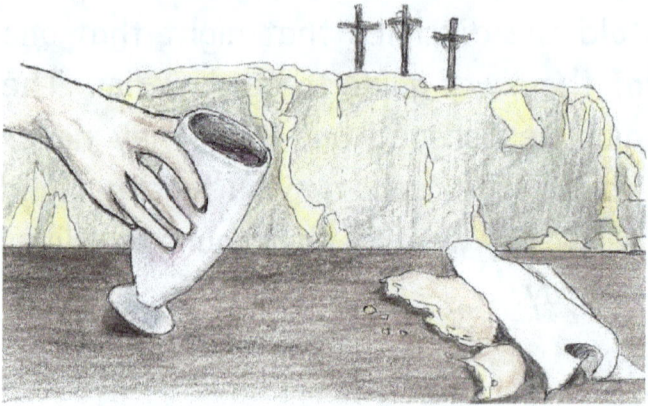

Application for Life:

My church has the Lord's Supper once every three months. It is also called Communion. It is a time to get things right with God and others. You take the bread and juice in remembrance of Jesus' sacrifice for us. I'm not sure if the disciples understood what was happening or not but this had to be such an overwhelming time of sadness for our Lord. I cannot thank Him enough for what He did for me.

Jesus Prays in Gethsemane

Background- Matthew 26:36-46; Mark 14:32-42; Luke 22:39-46; John 18:1-2

Jesus took Peter, James, and John to the garden of Gethsemane to pray. Jesus told his disciples to keep watch while He went further into the garden. Jesus was heavily burdened about what was to come. He prayed to God, His father, "If it is possible, take this cup from me: nevertheless, not what I will but what Thou wilt." Jesus went back to the disciples and found them asleep. He asked Peter why they couldn't pray and keep watch for an hour. Jesus prayed in agony. The sweat from His brow fell like great drops of blood to the ground. Again, he returned to find the disciples sleeping. This happened three times. The third time, Jesus told them to go ahead and sleep. The hour is come where I will be betrayed to man. He knew what God wanted done and He willingly obeyed.

Memory Verse- Psalm 55:17

Evening and morning and at noon will I pray and cry aloud; and He shall hear my voice.

Application for Life:

Jesus gave us the example of praying to God. It tells of Jesus praying often in the Bible. He wanted us to pray, too. We should thank God for all He does for us, pray for healing, pray for the joys in our life, and continually seek God's guidance in all we do and say. Even though Jesus did not get the answer He was hoping for. He willingly obeyed God. Thank You God for sending Your Son to earth so He could take away our sins.

Judas Betrays Jesus

Background- Matthew 26:1-5, 14-16,
47-56, 27:3-10; Mark 14:1-2, 10-11,
43-52; Luke 22:1-6, 47-53;
John 18:3-11

Judas Iscariot was one of Jesus' disciples. He decided to betray Jesus and went to the chief priests. They told Judas they would give him thirty pieces of silver. Judas told the chief priests that when he kissed the man on the cheek that it would be Jesus. Judas and a group of soldiers with swords went to the garden where Jesus and the disciples were praying. Judas kissed Jesus on the cheek. The soldiers came and took hold of Jesus. Peter was angry. He took his sword and cut off the ear of a soldier. Jesus said, "Put away thy sword. This is happening so the scriptures can be fulfilled." Jesus healed the soldier's ear. The soldiers then took Jesus away. Peter followed from afar to see what was going to happen. Judas took the money back to the chief priests and told them that he had sinned against an innocent man and he no longer wanted any part of Jesus' arrest. The chief priests said they wouldn't take his money back. Judas threw the money down and went out and hanged himself.

Memory Verse- Matthew 17:22b

The Son of Man shall be betrayed into the hands of men.

Application for Life:

It's hard to believe that one of the disciples could ever betray Jesus. They were the ones that got to be with Him daily hearing Him preach, seeing Him heal, and showing them how to live an obedient life for God. It just goes to show you how the devil can tempt us. The devil will do anything to keep us away from Jesus. We all sin but if we know Jesus as our Savior, we can be forgiven of those sins. Staying in prayer, reading God's Word daily, and having a heart that loves the Lord are the only ways to escape the devil's grip. Sometimes when I feel tempted, I like to stomp the floor and shout, "Get away from me, Satan. I belong to Jesus."

Peter Denies Jesus

Background- Matthew 26:31-38, 54-
62; Mark 14:27-31, 66-72;
Luke 22:31-38, 54-62; John 13:31-38,
18:15-18, 25-27

In one story, we learned how one
of the disciples, Judas Iscariot,
betrayed Jesus. In today's story, we
will see yet another disciple turn from
Jesus and deny ever knowing Him.
Jesus told His disciples they would all
flee from Him. Peter said that he
would never leave Jesus. Jesus said,
"Before the cock crows twice, you will
deny me three times."

After Jesus was taken by the
soldiers, Peter followed them. He hid
in the crowd. Some people in the
crowd starting saying, "Hey, you were
with Jesus. You are one of them."
Peter denied knowing Jesus three

times. He heard the rooster crow twice. Peter remembered what Jesus had told him. Peter cried bitterly. He was sorry for not standing up for Jesus.

This isn't the end of Peter's story though. Stay tuned for more on this disciple's life.

Memory Verse- Matthew 10:33

But whosoever shall deny me before men, him will I also deny before my Father which is in heaven.

Application for Life:

First betrayed and now denied. Jesus sure had problems with His disciples. We are His disciples today. Have you ever betrayed or denied Jesus to others? I hope that you and I would be willing to stand up for Jesus no matter what was thrown at us. It can be hard, especially when peers are cruel or bullies, to have the courage to stand up for Jesus. Just remember that God can help us overcome anything this world has to throw at us. Pray for His strength, listen to His guidance, and know He is with you always in everything you face. Be like David facing Goliath, Daniel facing the lions, or Esther facing the death of her people. Trust God, put your faith in Him, and let Him lead you.

Jesus' Trial and Sentence

Background- Matthew 27:11-26;
Mark 15:2-15; Luke 23:1-25;
John 18:28-40, 19:1-16

After the soldiers captured Jesus, they took Him to Pontius Pilate, the governor, for trial and sentencing. During the Passover feast, Pilate would release one of the prisoners. He asked the crowd to choose which prisoner to let go. The chief priests and Jewish officials had persuaded the crowd to ask for Barabbas, a murderer. When Pilate asked the crowd who to release, they shouted "Barabbas". Pilate asked the crowd what they wanted done with Jesus. The crowd shouted, "Crucify Him. Crucify Him." Pilate took a bowl of water and washed his hands in front of the crowd. He said to the crowd,

"I am innocent of the blood of this good man. The responsibility is yours." The crowd shouted, "We take responsibility. Crucify Him." Pilate released Barabbas to the crowd and sent Jesus with the soldiers to be crucified.

Memory Verse- Isaiah 53:5

But He was wounded for our transgressions, He was bruised for our iniquities: the chastisement of our peace was upon Him; and with His stripes we are healed.

Application for Life:

Can you believe that the followers of Jesus asked for a murderer to be released instead of the Messiah? I can't, even though I know what God planned so that we might live. These things, as awful as they were, had to happen so that we would have a way to live in heaven one day.

Jesus' Crucifixion and Burial

Background- Matthew 27:32-56;
Mark 15:21-41; Luke 23:26-49;
John 19:17-37

The Roman soldiers beat Jesus. They put a scarlet robe on Him and a crown on His head made from long thorns. They mocked Him calling Him, "King of the Jews." They made Jesus carry His own cross to Golgotha, the place of the skull, where He would be crucified. When Jesus fell from the weight of the cross, the soldiers got Simon of Cyrene to carry it for Him. When they reached Golgotha, the soldiers nailed Jesus to the cross. After hours of agony, Jesus died. It became dark all over the land. The veil in the temple was torn in two pieces. This veil had separated the Holy of Holies, God's Holy place, in the temple.

This meant that Jesus' death had made a way for us to see God one day. There was also an earthquake.

Joseph of Arimathea came and asked Pilate for Jesus' body so he could bury Jesus. Joseph wrapped Jesus' body in clean cloths and placed Jesus in the tomb he had bought for himself. A great stone was rolled in front of the door. Soldiers were put there to guard the tomb so Jesus' disciples could not steal the body and say He was alive.

Memory Verse- John 3:17

For God sent not His Son into the world to condemn the world; but that the world through Him might be saved.

Application for Life:

What a sad story this is!!! Jesus, the Messiah, was crucified on a cross. I cannot possibly imagine the agony Jesus went through just to save us. I hope you have accepted this gift Jesus gave us. By asking Jesus to be your Savior and Lord, you are giving yourself eternal life with Him and God the Father. Without Jesus being willing to die for us, we would not have that. Thank You Jesus and Father God for loving the world enough to sacrifice Your life for ours.

Jesus is Alive

Background- Matthew 28:1-7; Mark 16:1-11; Luke 24:1-12; John 20:1-18

The last story was very sad but now for "the rest of the story." You heard me right. That was NOT the end of the story of Jesus. Some of the women who followed Jesus were going to the tomb to put perfumes on the body and get Him ready for burial. When they arrived, the soldiers were on the ground and the stone was rolled away from the tomb. They entered the tomb and an angel of the Lord said, "Be not afraid. You are looking for Jesus. He is not here. He is risen." The angel told the women to go and tell Peter and the others that Jesus was alive, and they would see Him soon. Jesus first appeared to Mary Magdalene of whom He had cast out seven demons. She went and told Jesus' followers that He was alive, and she had seen Him.

Memory Verse- Matthew 28:6a

He is not here: for He is risen as He said.

Application for Life:

Hallelujah!!! The Easter story was very sad, but we can be glad to know that Jesus is alive. Jesus lives in heaven with God and we will get to meet Him one day if we have accepted Him as our Savior and Lord. I love happy endings (sniff! sniff!) Yes, I am crying but they are tears of joy. Hope you've experienced those tears of joy, too, when you came to know Jesus. We'll be together in eternity praising God and Jesus singing, "Holy, Holy, Holy is the Lord God Almighty." See you there.

Emmaus Road

Background- Luke 24:13-34

After Jesus had risen from the grave, He began showing Himself to others. One day, two of His followers were traveling to Emmaus just outside Jerusalem. The two men were talking about the death of Jesus. Jesus began walking with them, but they didn't realize it was Him. Jesus asked them what they were so upset about. One of the men, named Cleopas, told Him the terrible things that had happened. Jesus said, "Foolish people. Is it so hard to believe what the scriptures told you would happen? The prophets told what must happen so that everyone had the chance to see glory." The two men invited Jesus to supper. They sat down to eat. Jesus broke the bread. The two men realized it had been Jesus walking with them. He disappeared. The men went back to Jerusalem to tell the others. When they arrived, the other followers said He had appeared to Peter. Jesus really is alive.

Memory Verse- Acts 8:32

The place of the scripture which he read was this, He was led as a sheep to the slaughter; and like a lamb dumb before His shearer, so opened He not His mouth.

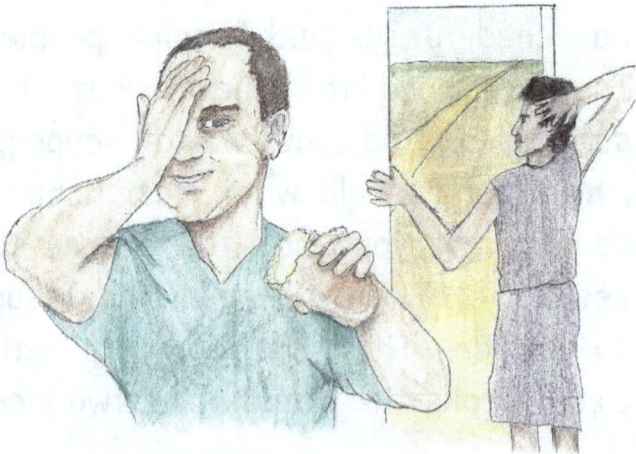

Application for Life:

Can you imagine walking down the road with your friend and Jesus joins you. That would be exciting. If you know Jesus and accept Him as your Savior, then one day that will happen. Jesus wanted His followers to know that He had risen, just like He said He would. Jesus appeared before His followers after the resurrection (rising from the dead) to bring glory to God the Father.

Jesus Appears to Disciples

Background- Mark 16:12-14;
Luke 24:35-43; John 20:19-29

Jesus appeared to His ten of His disciples after He had risen from death. The disciples were afraid. Jesus told them to look at the nail scars in His hands and feet and know it was Him. Thomas had not been with the others. When they told him, he didn't believe them. Jesus appeared again when Thomas was there and said, "Thomas, touch the scars in my hands and the place in my side where the sword went through." Thomas did and said, "I do believe it is You Lord." Jesus said, "Thomas, you believe because you have seen me: blessed are they that have not seen but yet believed." Jesus opened the eyes and ears of the disciples to understand the scriptures. Jesus knew He would not be on earth much longer and wanted them to be His witnesses all over the world. He led the disciples to Bethany and blessed them. He ascended (taken up) into heaven. The disciples were in the temple continually praising and blessing God.

Memory Verse- Hebrews 11:1

Now faith is the substance of things hoped for, the evidence of things not seen.

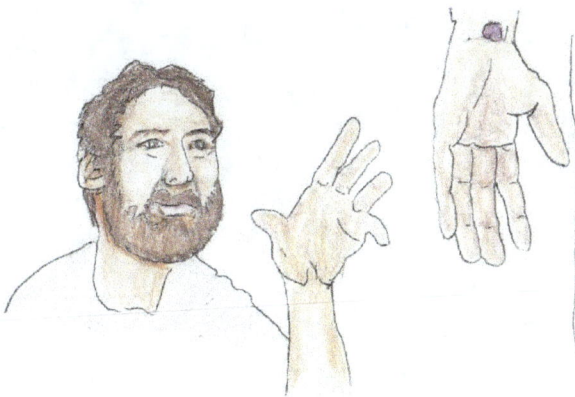

Application for Life:

I am so glad I was raised by Christian parents who taught me to have faith- to believe without seeing. I'm sure that Thomas believed in Jesus but not that He had risen. He wanted to "see" Him and touch His nail-pierced hands. Jesus appeared again to the disciples when Thomas was there just so Thomas could "see" Him. Jesus made it clear though that the people who believe without seeing will be blessed. I'm looking forward to that day, aren't you?

Jesus Challenges Peter

Background- John 21:15-23

Jesus had shown Himself to His disciples several times since He had risen from the dead. One time when they were eating together, Jesus spoke to Peter. "Simon, do you love Me?" Peter answered, "Yes Lord. You know I love You." Jesus replied, "Feed my sheep." Jesus said that second time, "Simon, do you love Me?" Simon responded, "Yes Lord, You know I love You." Jesus told him, "Feed my lambs." The third time Jesus asked, "Simon, do you love Me?" Peter was so sad. He said, "Lord, You know all things so You must know that I love You." Jesus said, "Feed my sheep."

Jesus was not talking about real sheep but about people. Jesus was telling Peter to go and preach to others and tell them about Jesus and how to be saved.

Some people say that Jesus asked Peter three times to take away the three times that Peter denied Him before He was crucified. You can decide what you think on that subject.

Memory Verse- Matthew 28:19-20

Go ye therefore and teach all nations, baptizing them in the name of the Father, and of the Son, and of the Holy Ghost. Teaching them to observe all things whatsoever I commanded you: and lo, I am with you always, even unto the end of the world.

Application for Life:

The memory verse today is called The Great Commission. Jesus said it to His disciples so they would tell others when He ascended into heaven. If we are believers, we are to be His witnesses today. We may not be preachers or missionaries, but we can tell our family, friends, neighbors, and people we meet. In the next story, you'll see how the disciples met hardships for preaching but continued any way. I hope you and I can be that brave as we tell others about Jesus and how they can have Him as Savior and Lord of their life.

The Disciples Preach

Background- Acts 2:14-42, 3:12-26,
8:4-40, 12:6-19, 13:1-43, 14:1-28,
16:1-40, 17:1-34

Peter, Paul, Barnabus, Silas, and Phillip were some of the followers of Jesus that traveled to many places to preach. They were persecuted, beaten, put into prison, and even threatened to be killed. They did not care because there were also people wherever they preached that believed in Jesus and were saved.

Once when Herod had arrested Peter, he had Peter put in chains and put soldiers to guard him. That night, the angel of the Lord came and shone a bright light. The angel told Peter to get up and go. Peter stood up and the chains fell off. As Peter and the angel ran out, the large iron gate at the entrance opened by itself. Peter knew that God had sent the angel to get him away from Herod and the ones who wanted to kill Him. Peter ran to Mary's house (she was the mother of Mark). Peter knocked on the door. The servant girl, Rhoda, answered the door. She was so shocked to see Peter at the door that she closed the door in his face. She ran back to tell the others gathered in the house. They asked her where he was or that maybe she had seen an angel. Peter kept knocking and they finally let him in. The crowd had gathered at the house to pray for Peter to be released from prison. Peter told them the angel of the Lord had been sent to save him.

Another time, Phillip saw an Ethiopian man reading the scriptures. He was reading from the Old Testament book of Isaiah. Phillip asked the Ethiopian man, "Do you understand what you are reading?" The Ethiopian man said, "No. There is no one to teach me." Phillip began explaining what the scriptures said and told him about Jesus. When they came to a body of water, the Ethiopian man asked Phillip to baptize him.

There are so many wonderful stories about the disciples preaching that I couldn't write them all. Be sure to read more of them. You can find more in the background references.

Memory Verse- Mark 16:15

And He said unto them, "Go ye into all the world and preach the gospel to every creature."

Application for Life:

I hope that I would be like Peter and Phillip and the other followers of Jesus and continue to tell others about Jesus even if I were being persecuted, put in prison, beaten, or even threatened to be killed. I know it would be scary, but I know my God will take care of me in every situation. I hope you will learn to put your faith and trust in Jesus. No matter what you face, He is on your side.

The Disciples Heal
Background- Acts 3:1-11, 9:32-43

The disciples were given the power of healing in Jesus' name after Jesus ascended into heaven. Peter healed a crippled man that begged at the gate. The crippled man saw Peter and asked for money. Peter said, "Silver and gold have I none, but in the name of Jesus rise up and walk." The crippled man leaped up and began praising God. There was also a woman, named Dorcas, who was a believer and did many good things for others. She died. Peter came to the room where Dorcas was. He said, "Dorcas, arise." She opened her eyes and sat up. Many people believed in Jesus when they heard that Peter had raised Dorcas from the dead. One other time, Peter healed a lame man who had been sick in bed for eight years. All the people in Lydda and Sharon that saw the lame man walking came to know Jesus as their Savior and Lord.

Memory Verse- Matthew 10:1

And when He had called unto Him His twelve disciples, He gave them power against unclean spirits, to cast them out, and to heal all manner of sickness and all manner of disease.

Application for Life:

I believe God gives healing even today. We can ask for healing in prayer. I have seen people healed when prayer was the only thing that could have brought healing. I am a strong believer in prayer, not just for healing. I talk to God about everything. He already knows my thoughts, but He loves to listen to His children. Go to Him in prayer and thank Him, praise Him, ask Him for what you need or want, and especially ask for healing. Just remember that not all prayers are answered the way we want them to be. Only God knows what is ahead and what's best. It's human to question why something happens but trust God- He loves you and He'll carry you through anything.

Saul on the Road to Damascus
Background- Acts 9:1-31

There was a man named Saul who persecuted the Jews and any believers of Jesus. He was traveling to Damascus to take prisoners of the Jews and followers of Jesus. On his way, he was blinded by a bright light. The Lord asked Saul why he was persecuting Him. Saul asked who was speaking to him. Jesus said, "It is Jesus, the one you are persecuting." Saul asked Jesus what He wanted him to do. Jesus told Saul to go into town and it would be revealed to him. Saul was still blind, so his men had to lead him into Damascus.

In Damascus, there was a man named Ananias. The Lord spoke to him in a vision and told him to help Saul. Ananias was afraid. He didn't want to go. The Lord told Ananias not to be afraid and that Saul was chosen to be a witness of Jesus to all people. Ananias went to Saul, placed his hands on his eyes, restored Saul's sight, and filled him with the Holy Ghost. Saul could see. He immediately went to be baptized.

Saul later changed his name to Paul. He became a great preacher and witness for Jesus.

Memory Verse- 1 John 1:7

But if we walk in the Light as He is in the light, we have fellowship one with another and the blood of Jesus Christ His Son cleanseth us from all sin.

Application for Life:

Can you imagine a light so bright that you are blinded? I bet Saul was afraid. He had been the bad guy and now he was in for some eye-opening news about his life. God can take even the worst person and turn them into a great witness for Him. That's just what He did for Saul. We need to leave the judging of others to God. We don't see what God does. We, as humans, see the outside and actions of others. God sees the heart and possibilities in us all.

109

Put on the Whole Armor of God
Background- Ephesians 6:10-20

One of my favorite passages in the Bible is when Paul (yes, the same Saul that once persecuted Jews but was saved on the road to Damascus) wrote a letter to the church in Ephesus. He was trying to encourage them to be courageous and strong in their lives and live for the Lord. Here is the way Paul said we should "dress".

Put on the whole armor of God so you can stand up against the devil. Put on the strong belt of truth, the breastplate of righteousness, shoes that give you speed to spread the Word of God, shield of faith, a helmet of salvation, a sword of the Spirit- God's Word, and pray continually.

Memory Verse- Ephesians 6:11

Put on the whole armor of god that ye may be able to stand against the wiles of the devil.

Application for Life:

I read my Bible daily, pray, have faith, and am saved by the grace of God. Even having the armor of God on, it is still hard to fight the devil and all the temptations he throws our way. Without the armor, we would have no hope to win against the devil. Daily put on your armor and the Lord will help you fight the devil.

Jesus is Coming Again

Background- Revelations 1-22

I'll be honest, the book of Revelation is very difficult to understand. It is filled with lots of symbolism which makes it hard. I have been through many studies with pastors and still have not grasped it all. What I do want to share from this book is the promises made to us when we die if we are a believer in Jesus Christ. As I did for the final story in the Old Testament book, I am ending with a poem. Hope you enjoy learning about Revelation in this way.

<u>Jesus is Coming Again</u>

Master, Savior, King of Kings,

Most Holy, Lord of Everything.

Creator before time began,

Light of the World, Prince of Peace, Son of Man.

Alpha, Omega, Beginning, and End,

First and Last, Protector, and Friend.

Eternal Son, Living Water, and Lamb,

Bread of Life, Messiah, Redeemer, I AM.

Jesus went to prepare a home in heaven for us.

One day He'll return on a great, white horse

to get all the believers who have not died before

or to let you reign during the battles for the world.

There will be a time of tribulation- the last chance to accept Jesus as Lord.

Satan, false prophets, and the Antichrist will try to get you to listen to their words.

But the Lord will make the final judgement call.

Is your name in the Book of Life or not at all?

If you accepted Jesus as your Savior one day,

then your mansion in glory is already paid.

With great walls of jasper and precious jewels everywhere.

Gates of pearl and streets of gold, transparent and clear.

Our mansions in heaven are awaiting you and me.

We can live eternally praising our King.

Holy, holy, holy, Lord God Almighty.

Worthy is the Lamb to receive power and honor and glory.

We praise You Lord, keep us faithful and true

on earth until we join believers in heaven praising You.

Memory Verse- 1 Corinthians 2:9

But as it is written, eye hath not seen nor ear heard, neither have entered into the heart of man, the things which God hath prepared for them that love Him.

Application for Life:

Jesus is the same yesterday, today, and forever. The Revelation may be difficult to understand and a little scary. If you know Jesus as your Lord and Savior, you have nothing to worry about. He will take care of you until it is time for you to join Him in your mansion in heaven. I hope you continue to study the Bible- God's Word- the two-edged sword that gives you protection against the devil and his followers. Seek Jesus and follow Him only. Your rewards in heaven cannot be surpassed on this earth we live on.

In closing, I just wanted to thank you for reading my Bible stories. I hope they have made a difference in your life. Continue to study God's Word daily and learn more. May God richly bless you in your life here on earth. If you are His child, I know you will be blessed in heaven.

Your friend in Him, Victoria Fletcher

P.S. You can see other books I have written on my website: victoriafletcher.biz

www.ingramcontent.com/pod-product-compliance
Lightning Source LLC
LaVergne TN
LVHW021133080426
835509LV00010B/1344